HELP MY CHILD HAS
TYPE 1 DIABETES

HELP MY CHILD HAS
TYPE 1 DIABETES

ADVICE, INFORMATION, AND REAL STORIES FOR PARENTS AND CARERS

ROXANA REYNOLDS

authorHOUSE®

AuthorHouse™ UK Ltd.
1663 Liberty Drive
Bloomington, IN 47403 USA
www.authorhouse.co.uk
Phone: 0800.197.4150

Published by AuthorHouse   04/25/2014

ISBN: 978-1-4969-7778-6 (sc)
ISBN: 978-1-4969-7815-8 (hc)
ISBN: 978-1-4969-7779-3 (e)

Roxana is not a trained medical professional, nutritionist, or dietician. All information is
from personal experience and years of learning from books and the Internet. The advice offered
in this book is not intended to be a substitute for the advice of your diabetes clinic or GP.

Foreword

Roxie always looks after her health, aiming to do the best she can despite coping with the challenges of having type 1 diabetes since 2000. As Roxie's diabetes dietician and insulin pump specialist, I have known her for five years, and more closely since she progressed onto insulin pump therapy in 2009. She was very reluctant to try this new technology but worked diligently to get to know the systems, develop her skills, and optimise her diabetes control, and this has paid off with improvements to her control and quality of life.

She is also totally dedicated to supporting her son Eddie, who also has type 1 diabetes, to learning along the way, and to optimising his control with all the tools available to them.

Roxie's dedication is also shown in this book, which she has written with the aim of offering personalised patient guidance to other parents of children with type 1 diabetes, incorporating practical tips and reassurance.

Helping others to do the best for their children with diabetes shows Roxie's caring and passionate nature.

Well done, Roxie!

Emma Jenkins

Acknowledgements

This book wouldn't have come about if my precious son Eddie hadn't been diagnosed with type 1 diabetes. Having a child with diabetes taught me patience, gave me strength, and above all, gave me the wisdom to learn all I could.

Knowledge has been the key to ensuring that I gave Eddie the best care possible. Together we have ridden the diabetes roller coaster. We have had a few bumpy rides and occasionally felt like we would fall off, but together we've held on tight, and in doing so, we've discovered a very special bond.

My acknowledgements wouldn't be complete without mentioning my best friend, my husband, Steve. Thank you for our life together. Thank you to David, my first born, when I truly believed in magic. You have grown up to be such a loving, generous, gorgeous son. Thank you for coming into my world.

Thank you, Emma Jenkins, a lovely part of my diabetes team, for reading my book to check all the medical jargon.

Thank you to all the mums and dads on my Facebook page that have contributed real stories and pictures of our type 1 children.

Mum, I love you, and yes, I've checked my spelling and grammar.

Learn from yesterday,
Live for today,
Hope for tomorrow. —*Albert Einstein*

Introduction

Type 1 diabetes is five times more common than meningitis. Diagnosis of type 1 diabetes is usually delayed, and 30 per cent of newly diagnosed children have at least one related medical condition, for example gastroenteritis, when the child is vomiting. To differentiate the child will also be urinating a lot.

In some cases, medical professionals miss early warning signs, resulting in children becoming seriously ill with diabetic ketoacidosis (DKA) or, in rare cases, dying. When cells in the body don't get the glucose they need for energy, then the body burns fat, which produces ketones. These are acids that build up in the blood, and they are extremely toxic. This ketone build-up is a warning that you are sick or that diabetes is out of control.

Do you know the symptoms of type 1?

- excessive thirst
- bed-wetting, even for previously dry children
- frequent urination
- oral or genital thrush
- weight loss
- abdominal pain
- vomiting

- blurred vision
- lethargy

If DKA has already set in, then the child will usually vomit, have laboured or rapid breathing, and have abdominal pain.

If your child has any of these symptoms, then he or she must go to the hospital or doctor's surgery immediately. A doctor will do a simple finger prick and use a blood-glucose testing strip to determine whether the child's blood glucose level is high. To detect ketones, the doctor may test the child's urine with a urine strip or ketone meter.

Why I wrote this book

I decided to write this book because I know firsthand how frightening it is to have a child diagnosed with type 1 diabetes. My son Eddie was diagnosed April 2000, at the tender age of two. Back then, there were no support groups, so I felt very isolated as I battled daily with a relentless disease that filled our lives and cast a dark shadow over my little boy. I scoured the Internet for information to ensure I could give my son the best quality of life, for I realised knowledge was power, knowledge was the key, and I eventually came to terms with the disease.

Years later, Facebook was born, and I set up a support page for parents called What Mums and Dads Need To Know To Help Children With Type 1 Diabetes. I couldn't believe how many children were being diagnosed with diabetes—about 1 in every 450 children, most of them with type 1. There was a lot of ignorance surrounding this disease, so I decided I could help other vulnerable parents by educating them on a social network page. I am not a medical expert, but being type 1 myself and having a child with type 1 gave me firsthand knowledge to share with other parents. Even so, I am always learning something new every day.

I know only too well how scary a diagnosis is in the beginning—how it brings your emotions to the fore and how the stress of it can strain relationships. Yes, it is hard, yes, it is relentless, but you and your child can live with diabetes. You can walk alongside it rather than cower under its shadow.

Diabetes can be confusing and complicated and all the medical information daunting to say the least! But I hope I can help you take care of your child's diabetes every day without your feeling overwhelmed and out of your depth.

Diabetes cannot be ignored.
You have to learn about it.
You have to be organised.
You have to have a routine.

You may have to incorporate new foods into your child's diet, and you will need to be good at basic maths, as you'll have to work out insulin-to-carbohydrate ratios. Illness, exercise, and travel will constantly challenge you. I'm not going to lie—this illness never ends. You will despair at times, but it does get easier.

You are in charge.

CHAPTER 1

Eddie's Diagnosis

Eddie was diagnosed with type 1 diabetes when he was two, although I suspect he had probably had it a while.

In hindsight, it is very easy to spot the signs of diabetes, but when you're not considering it as a possibility, you can easily miss these symptoms. Eddie, a happy and mischievous little toddler, experienced a gradual, steady decline until one day he looked very ill. He was also listless, unresponsive, and excessively thirsty. I will never forget that day.

Because I'm diabetic, I had some sticks for testing the amount of glucose in the urine, which indicates the amount in the blood. A test of Eddie's urine gave such an extremely high blood-glucose reading that it was off the scale. I knew I had to call our doctor straightaway, and she came round immediately, at seven at night, and said that Eddie would have to be admitted to hospital.

My husband and I were mortified, as if a curse had been put on our son.

Once we arrived at the hospital, Eddie's blood-glucose level was higher than the highest reading on the meter—30! For comparison, a person without diabetes will have a blood glucose level between 4 and 7. I cannot describe the emotions my husband and I felt to hear our child's diagnosis. I had to stay in hospital with Eddie for three days until his sugars stabilised.

After the diagnosis and amidst the stress, a miracle happened, his sugar levels had lowered dramatically and Eddie no longer felt unwell. We got our smiling, cheeky little boy back and went away laden with insulin pens, meters, and information. Our son's life with diabetes had begun, and what a journey we've had.

The thirteen years since then have been a roller-coaster ride. Coping with this illness is scary as glucose levels fluctuate, sometimes becoming either too low (hypoglycaemia) or too high (hyperglycaemia). We faced constant testing and worrying that Eddie's levels could go low in the night and that he could go in a coma. It was relentless. We have had good times, too. Eddie has grown up healthy and has no psychological problems due to his diabetes.

He says, "I am a normal boy who just has to inject."

With knowledge and understanding, we found it possible to take control of our lives and cope with this disease.

CHAPTER 2

What Is Type 1 Diabetes?

Type 1 diabetes, also known as juvenile or insulin-dependent diabetes, usually develops in children and young adults. The disease develops quickly over days or weeks as the pancreas stops making insulin. Then, it is treated with insulin either by injection or from an insulin pump. Keeping blood-sugar levels under control is paramount to ensure that complications, which can have long-term effects, don't occur, and this is done by doing regular blood tests (finger pricking) every day.

Educating others

There is a lot of ignorance surrounding diabetes, so here are some of the questions Eddie and I have encountered:

Why does the pancreas stop working?

Type 1 diabetes is considered to be an *autoimmune disease*, which means that the immune system makes antibodies to attack bacteria, viruses and germs.

People that have type 1 diabetes make antibodies that attach themselves to the beta cells in the pancreas. These are thought to destroy the cells that make insulin.

Does it hurt?

Poking ourselves with needles, either to inject insulin or to do a blood test, can sometimes hurt.

You can't eat that—you're diabetic!

Actually, we can eat whatever we like as long as we have the right insulin dose. The best diet for us is a healthy, balanced diet, the same that's recommended for everyone!

Did you get diabetes from eating too many cakes and biscuits?

No, that is not the cause of type 1 diabetes. We did nothing to cause it.

Will you grow out of it?

We wish! No, we will have it all our lives.

Can you get rid of it by exercising and eating a healthy diet?

Type 1 diabetes is not caused by poor diet or being overweight (these are associated with type 2 diabetes). Just like they are for anyone, exercise and a healthy diet are important, but, unfortunately, type 1 diabetes will not go away whatever we do.

Are you sure you can play football, tennis, or badminton or go rock climbing or surfing?

We can play *all* sports and do anything else we want as long as we adjust our insulin accordingly.

CHAPTER 3

The Reality of Diagnosis

Learning your child has diabetes is, without a doubt, a traumatic event for any family. When Eddie was first diagnosed, we went through the classic stages of grief: anger, denial, depression, resolution, and, finally, acceptance.

The early days after diagnosis are the worst, as parents face significant responsibilities and emotional, mental, and physical pressures. Having a child with type 1 can cause extreme stress between couples, as both parents may lack confidence in their ability to help and in their knowledge of what to do. At this stage, you need support from your diabetes clinic, your family, and your friends. Don't be afraid to ask for it. You can also seek out support groups online or in your local area.

Wherever your child goes, whether it is to a nursery, to school, or to out-of-school activities, all adults there will need to know how to take care of your child when you're not around.

Adjusting to a diagnosis can take you six to nine months, and depending on your child's age, it may take him or her longer.

The fact that your child depends on you naturally puts you under a lot of pressure. You can only do your best. Ask for help from your diabetes specialist nurse, a good friend, or others. Learn all you can, as knowledge will give you confidence. Remember, too, to take some time out for yourself. When Eddie was a toddler, I shared all the basic diabetes facts with a good friend, and she helped me with everything, including giving Eddie his insulin. This help gave me the opportunity to escape, even if only for an hour.

It is a lonely road, and you will be in a dark place for a while. You may cry, feel frustrated, feel angry, and ask, "Why my child?" If you seriously can't cope, please seek help from your GP. Don't suffer in silence.

After your child's diagnosis, people's perceptions of you may change because of their lack of knowledge. Share all the information you've learned with your immediate family and friends to help them overcome their ignorance, and correct people when they make silly comments about your child's diabetes.

Above all, be positive. Empower yourself, raise awareness, and speak to other parents in the same position.

Very young children won't understand what diabetes is or why you're injecting them. In time they'll learn from you, your diabetes nurses, and other medical consultants, but until then, they'll rely on you for care and reassurance. Your child trusts you, so you owe it to him or her to be strong and knowledgeable. As you gain understanding, you'll gain more confidence, and you'll pass both on to your child, paving the way for a positive future.

CHAPTER 4

Diagnosis: Real Stories

Told by Donna Hoskins

My nearly three-year-old Ellyse had been ill for a few days with a temperature and was generally feeling unwell. She was back in nappies after being dry for six months and was drinking fifteen or more four-hundred-millilitre bottles of squash a day. Her breathing was also heavy, and she just seemed to lack energy. I took her to see our GP and told him all this. He first said that it was a virus but then gave my daughter antibiotics for a water infection.

Four days later my daughter hadn't picked up at all and refused to walk, saying that her legs hurt. By this point her breathing was terrible. I had another GP look her over, and she said that she believed my daughter had an ear, throat, and lung infection; gave her stronger antibiotics; and said to bring her back in four days.

The following day my daughter was unresponsive, wouldn't eat or drink, and clearly had serious trouble breathing. We rushed her to A&E, and doctors rushed her straight to the resuscitation room.

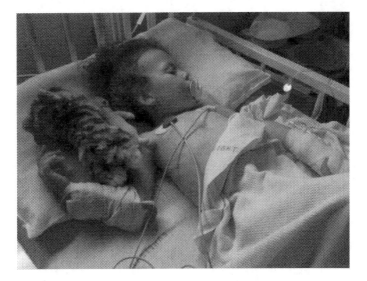

I was told she had type 1 diabetes, that she was in a semi-coma because of DKA, and that she would be dependent on insulin for the rest of her life.

The doctor asked me how long she had been poorly and whether I had taken her to see a doctor. I explained that my daughter had seen two GPs in a week, and the A&E doctor was gobsmacked that both GPs had misdiagnosed her when an A&E nurse could know she had type 1 diabetes just by looking at her.

Jak's diagnosis
Told by Leanne Willet

Our journey with diabetes began back in April 2009, when Jak was two years old. We were on a family holiday in Turkey at the time, and on the last Thursday of the holiday, we decided to spend the day at the beach with the children. After playing for a few hours, Jak came to me and said his head hurt. I guessed he had probably had a bit too much sun and thought it best to return to the apartment. Once there, Jak went to sleep, but he woke around thirty minutes later and was sick. I didn't think too much of it and still thought it was just a case of too much sun.

The following day, Friday, Jak was as boisterous as ever playing around and doing what two-year-olds do, but he vomited after eating. I still put it down to sunstroke. I also noticed that Jak was drinking a lot more and, consequently, urinating more. However, with no history of diabetes in the family, I had no idea of the symptoms, so I put this behaviour down to the extremely hot weather and so continued with our holiday.

On Saturday, Jak was still vomiting and slept quite a lot through the day. I realised then he possibly had something other than sunstroke, but only a bit of holiday tummy, possibly because he had eaten something in Turkey that hadn't agreed with him. As we were flying home the next night, Jak's dad and I agreed that if he was still vomiting when we got home to the UK, we would take him to his doctor's.

In the meantime, we went to a Turkish chemist and bought some anti-nausea medicine to see us over and called NHS for advice, only to be told that they would not put us through to speak to anyone, as we were not in the UK (apparently they can only advise if you are on British soil).

Jak shared a room with us that night. At about 3 a.m., he woke up and asked for something to drink. After having his drink, he went straight back to sleep, but for some reason, I couldn't settle in. Jak's being ill for a few days played on my mind. After tossing and turning for about an hour, I turned on the light and went to wake Jak, only to find that he wouldn't wake up. Fortunately, a hospital was five hundred yards from our apartment, and we literally ran there with Jak in our arms.

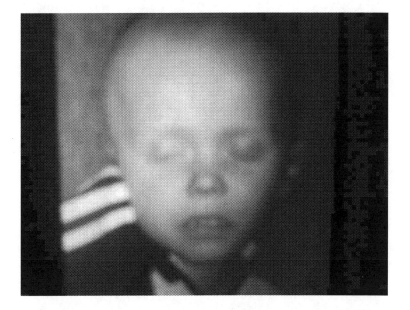

Once at the hospital, it was all action. The doctors thought Jak was severely dehydrated and spent the next two and a half hours trying to find a vein that hadn't collapsed to get an IV line into him. In the end, the only option was to get a line into his neck, as he was deteriorating fast. Eventually the hospital personnel managed to get blood and other fluids from him and ran tests to find out the exact cause of Jak's state. He was taken to a private room, and we sat there for around four hours until a doctor arrived with two people, one of whom was an interpreter. The doctor told us that Jak was in a critical condition and that his body was starting to shut down. The next things to be affected would be his heart or brain.

Although every parent imagines they'll fall apart at such news, all I remember is being completely numb except for a sick feeling and having to sit down before I fell down. The doctor transferred Jak to intensive care, where he was hooked up to all sorts of machines. At around this time, Jak's blood results came back: his blood sugar was 29 mmol/l. He was immediately hooked up to an insulin drip.

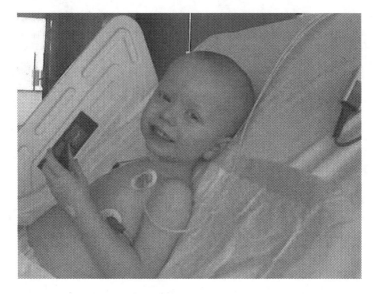

Eventually Jak could go back to England, and he was taken straight from the airport to Bolton Royal Hospital. The following day we left with leaflets, needles, blood-monitoring machines, and all the rest of the paraphernalia and our lives changed forever.

Georgia's diagnosis
Told by Jacqui Horsley

Georgia had been complaining of being hungry and having headaches for a number of weeks, maybe even months. She had lost weight, too, but we put that down to a growth spurt. Then she was always thirsty and visiting the toilet a lot more than usual. Alarm bells should have rung in my head, but she had been struck with a few urinary tract infections over the past year, so I just thought, *Oh no, not that again.* Then she began getting up in the night to go to the toilet and getting a glass of water to drink immediately after.

This behaviour became more frequent over the next two weeks, so I decided to look through my medical books. Diabetes did come up a few times as I researched the symptoms, but I thought that she would surely be ill if it was diabetes, and apart from the odd grumble about aches and pains and the urinary problem, she seemed fine, so I dismissed that possibility.

She looked tired, and clearly her disturbed nights from so many toilet visits were taking their toll, so I decided that another trip to the doctor's was in order. The doctor wasn't available, but a nurse was happy to take a urine sample.

We had just got home when the phone rang, and the nurse said in a very sympathetic voice, "I am so sorry, but we believe Georgia may be diabetic, as her urine tests are off the scale. You will need to bring her back to us right now for a blood test. And pack a bag, as you will be going on to the hospital after." The nurse paused. "What is Georgia doing now? Is she okay?"

I said, "Yes, she's dancing to music on MTV."

The nurse said, "Really? Can you see her from the phone? Please don't leave her on her own, as she could collapse at any moment."

I was watching my daughter, and she did look perfectly normal dancing in front of the television, and I thought, *They have got this so wrong. They'll find they've made a mistake and will give us some antibiotics or something.* I felt like someone had told me a story about someone else—I couldn't believe that this they thought this about my child.

When the nurse rang off, I started making phone calls. I phoned my parents to tell them the results and asked them to pick up my fourteen-year-old son from school. I then rang my husband. All he said was, "Are you sure? Diabetes?" I said, "Yes, diabetes. The bad kind."

Then, out of the corner of my eye, I saw my daughter in a flood of tears. In my worry about contacting everyone before our trip to hospital,

I had forgotten the one little person who most needed to be told what was happening. She sobbed her heart out.

Through her tears, Georgia looked at me and asked, "Am I going to die? You said on the phone to dad that I had die-betes. Does that mean I'll die?"

I just held her tight and said, "I don't know anything about diabetes, but we're going to go to hospital, and they will make you better. They may even find out they got it wrong." In truth, I had no idea what any of this meant, but I knew that I wasn't going to leave her side until we knew all there was to know.

We went to the doctor's, and he did a finger prick and confirmed that she needed help straightaway. The doctor arranged for us to go straight to the children's ward at the local hospital.

We were shocked and afraid. This was something we had no knowledge of, but we could tell by everyone's reactions that it was serious. Nurses tested Georgia again at the hospital and then gave her an insulin injection and told her to rest. She was silent and calm with a mix of fear and embarrassment.

My husband and I sat with her all evening and called family and friends to tell them where we were and what had happened. Everyone reacted with disbelief.

Then, after giving us a brief introduction to diabetes, the doctor told us to go home and keep an eye on Georgia.

My husband collapsed into sobs at various times that evening, feeling helpless and totally out of control, but I didn't shed a tear. I was shocked, but I had a job to do. I knew that if I let one tear escape, I would fold and be useless to Georgia. I needed to be stronger than ever and take this on. Diabetes wasn't going to take my little girl from me. I was going to learn everything there was to know and do all I could. Diabetes had a fight on its hands from me!

The next morning we had to go back to the hospital by 7 a.m. and before breakfast for another injection. Georgia was brighter and smiling, as always. We met her diabetic nurse, Nicky, who had the softest and most reassuring voice, and she promised to come out to see us at home later that day to explain how she would provide care. She also said she would show me how to inject Georgia! What?

Everyone knows how squeamish I am and that I faint at blood tests, and Nicky expected me to inject my child? Of course, there was no other option. People often say to me. "Oh, I don't know how you do it. I could never do that." Of course you would when it's your child.

When Nicky came out that afternoon, she explained it all, and I gave Georgia her first injection, into her leg. My hands shook and my heart raced, but it was like I was breathing life back into her.

That was five years ago, and Georgia is fifteen now. She has been doing her own injections, four times a day, for a couple of years now. It's as natural to her now as cleaning her teeth. She has been brave and courageous and brilliant through it all. She has never lost her smile or her positive attitude, and although I hate diabetes, it has brought Georgia and me closer together.

When Georgia was ten years of age, diabetes came to live with us and briefly took away her independence. I was her only source of survival as I reminded her to test her blood, check her scores, and acting accordingly; injected her day and night; and kept her positive.

My world fell apart when they handed me my broken child and said, "Sorry, there is no cure," but we haven't given up. We'll keep diabetes with us always, but we've put it in our back pockets, and it won't stop us doing the things we want to. Georgia makes me proud every day for doing everything that other kids do.

Nurse Nicky has been with us through it all and is still only a mobile call away whenever we need her. She is brilliant. None of us knows what the future holds for our children, but parents with diabetic children may find the future frightening because we're reminded how easily our children's condition can change. My advice is to get out there and enjoy life and to not let diabetes hold you back.

CHAPTER 5

Care after Diagnosis

If your child has been admitted to hospital, then the doctors and nurses should have given you a full but concise explanation of diabetes and all the necessary facts in writing. After you receive this, it will take time for everything to sink in. You'll be affected emotionally, and it will be hard to adjust to your new life initially. You'll even feel overwhelmed. This is normal.

After the diagnosis, you should also:

- Be seen by a paediatric diabetes specialist nurse (DSN).
- Be given information about support groups. You can also ask your diabetes clinic about them. Diabetes UK and the Juvenile Diabetes Research Foundation (JDRF)
- www.diabetes.org.uk
- www.jdrf.org.uk
- both have Facebook support groups and websites.

Be informed of how to claim a Disability Living Allowance. A non-means-tested, tax free benefit. You can find out more about this online under Works and Pensions. www.gov.uk/government/ . . . /department-for-work-pensions or look at Disability Living Allowance (DLA) on the Diabetes UK site which helps parents and carers to understand the application process.

- Be given information on how and where to inject your child and how to dispose of needles and finger-pricking lancets. These and sharps boxes are available with a prescription.
- Be advised when to test your child's blood glucose levels and ketones and how to interpret the tests.
- Be supplied with information on how insulin, food, exercise, and illness affect your child's blood glucose levels.
- Be given information about hypoglycaemia (hypo), why it happens, and how to treat it with Glucogel and Glucagon injections.
- Be told about the *honeymoon phase*, or the period shortly after diagnosis.
- Inform your GP and set up a meeting about it with your child's nursery or school.
- Be given a telephone number to call twenty-four hours a day for advice and help from your diabetes team. There are there to help, so use them.
- See the DSN, consultant paediatrician, and dietician frequently with your child. Initially this could be monthly. Eventually you and your child will visit the diabetes clinic only three or four times a year, depending on your child's circumstances.

Eventually, you'll become more confident, and hopefully your child will become more stable. Your DSN will continually support you.

Who will I see at the diabetes clinic?

- Consultant paediatrician
- Children's diabetes nurse
- Dietician
- Clinic nurses

The Annual Review

Once your child reaches ten, he or she will have a more thorough examination once a year in which he or she will have blood and urine tests and be screened for thyroid and coeliac diseases. Your child will also have to have an annual eye exam. Please look at 'what are the complications' for more information.

HbA1c

This is a measure of your child's average blood glucose level over three months. When your child's blood glucose levels rise, this means that more glucose molecules attach to the haemoglobin molecules on their red blood cells. These then stay attached until the red cell dies, and the life span of a red cell is about 120 days.

The HbA1c test is taken on blood from a simple finger prick or vein. This is usually done twice a year but may be done more often if your child needs extra help. The results are useful for your diabetes team to ensure your child's insulin dose is adequate and to review lifestyle factors such as diet and exercise.

Previously, results of the HbA1c were measured as percentages, but they are now measured in millimoles per mole (mmol/mol):

86-108 mmol/mol = 10-12%
64-86 mmol/mol = 8-10%
53 mmol/mol = 7% (This is the target for your child.)

If your child's HbA1c is above 108 mmol/mol, or 12 %, this is very high, and your child will require a lot of help and support. Keeping your child's HbA1c as close to 53 mmol/mol as possible reduces the chance of future complications.

Behavioural problems with young children

Sometimes, even though your child may seem able to cope with their diagnosis, they may rebel against diabetes. They may become hysterical during visits to the GP or diabetes clinic. If your child is too young to communicate effectively, then they will react physically to fear or other emotions. They may lash out at other children by hitting, pinching, pulling hair, or biting.

If your child's behaviour is really bad, then your child's consultant may refer them to a child psychologist. Although it is hard, the best thing to do is not to condone behavioural problems to happen and not to treat your child differently to a child without diabetes. That is, you have to show your child consequences for their unacceptable behaviour, otherwise, you'll create loads of problems in the future.

CHAPTER 6

What Is the Honeymoon Period?

Type 1 diabetes occurs when about 80 per cent of the body's insulin-producing cells are destroyed. That means that only 20 per cent are still available, and your child will need a small amount of additional insulin. This is the honeymoon period, and it is quite common for blood-glucose levels to be normal at this time.

At this stage, you must be in constant contact with your DSN for advice. *Do not stop insulin doses!* If you do, your child could develop DKA.

The honeymoon phase is a difficult time because it happens as you're trying to establish a routine to manage diabetes and learning about carbohydrate counting, correction doses, and background or basal and short-acting insulin. This period will last weeks, months, or, in extremely rare cases, years, but it doesn't last forever.

CHAPTER 7

Hyperglycaemia: High Blood-Glucose Levels

Trying to keep your child's blood glucose between 4 and 7 mmol,/l a fasting or pre-meal target close to the non-diabetic range, is extremely difficult. In Eddie's case, we aim to keep his levels out of the double digits.

The most common reasons for hyperglycaemia

- not enough insulin
- not enough exercise or less exercise than usual
- more food than usual or more sugary or foods or drinks than usual (such as after a birthday party and eating out)
- illness or infection
- excitement or stress

Symptoms of hyperglycaemia

Hyperglycaemia can be hard to detect, as your child will, in all likelihood, look fine. A couple of hours may pass after something that causes the condition, but then your child may be more thirsty than normal and will probably go to the toilet more than normal.

Bed-wetting can occur at night because of high blood-glucose levels. This was a problem with Eddie in his early years at primary school, as he was such a heavy sleeper.

If your child starts vomiting, complains of stomach pains, or feels lethargic, then your child may have developed ketones due to the lack of insulin.

If your child's blood glucose is high, then you must correct it with fast-acting insulin. Please consult your DSN for advice on correction doses.

Hyperglycaemia and ketones

High blood-glucose levels and ketones in the blood mixed with illness such as viruses, colds with temperatures or vomiting with a temperature equals ketoacidosis, which can be life-threatening. Ketones make the blood acidic, and can appear in the blood and urine if the body has insufficient insulin. Ketones are chemical by-products of the breakdown of fat. When the body can't use its glucose for energy because of lack of insulin, then the body burns fat for energy instead. Therefore, ketones are a warning sign for insufficient insulin. They can also appear if your child develops an infection or illness.

It is recommended that you test for ketones in your child's urine with strips or a ketone-testing meter. If ketones are present and your child's blood-glucose levels are high, you will have to test more often. Please be aware that some children can have ketones first thing in the morning even though the blood glucose level is not high. If the child isn't ill, then these ketones are usually *starvation ketones* that appear because the child hasn't eaten for several hours.

Warning signs of ketoacidosis

- increased thirst
- passing noticeably more urine than usual
- high blood-glucose levels
- presence of ketones in urine or blood
- vomiting or nausea
- stomach pains
- tiredness
- deep, rapid breathing
- sweet smell, like acetone or pear drops, on the breath (I can smell them, but not everyone can.)

Never miss your child's insulin, even if your child doesn't want to eat or is vomiting. If these conditions are present, the dose may need to change. Always call your diabetes clinic if you are in doubt.

If your child has a positive ketone test

- Give your child *double the dose* of rapid-acting insulin as soon as possible and every two hours if ketones are still present. Positive ketone tests *always* require treatment with extra insulin. Use your normal rapid-acting insulin.
- Get your child to drink plenty of fluid, either water or sugar-free drinks. This will stop dehydration and help to flush the ketones out of the system.
- Test blood glucose levels every one to two hours.
- Be vigilant, and seek treatment if necessary.
- Contact your diabetes team if high blood glucose and ketones persist.
- **Contact your GP or A&E department if** your child is vomiting, as dehydration can occur.
- Blood glucose is less than 4, with ketones of 0 to 2.9. If these are starvation ketones, treat the condition as hypoglycaemia and give fluids containing carbohydrates instead.
- Ketones are 3 or more
- You must test your child's blood or urine for ketones if the blood glucose is over 14 mmol/l
- Find the cause of your child's high blood glucose levels, and seek treatment or advice.
- Please note, this is only a guide!

CHAPTER 8

Hypoglycaemia: Low Blood-Glucose Levels

Hypoglycaemia, an episode of which is often called *a hypo*, means blood glucose levels are low, below 4 mmol/l.

What causes a hypo?

Hypos can occur for various reasons:

Your child may have had a delayed meal; too much insulin; been more active than usual; missed a snack or may even been unwell.

Symptoms

Children experience hypos differently, but in the main, they feel dizzy or light-headed, they make be shaking, they may have a headache, they may have clammy skin, or they may behave irrationally or seem moody and irritable. When Eddie has a hypo, he suddenly looks very pale, and sometimes he seems disorientated. When in doubt, test your child's blood-glucose level.

Hypos: A quick guide

Why is my child having a hypo?

- too much insulin
- unplanned or too much exercise
- delayed or missed meal
- not enough food.

Symptoms to watch out for

- hunger
- shakiness
- mood change
- lack of concentration
- sweating
- paleness

What to do in case of a hypo

Treat it immediately with something that raises blood glucose levels:

- Lucozade (100 ml)
- a small can (150 ml) of *non-diet* fizzy drink
- a small carton (200 ml) of orange juice
- 4-5 GlucoTabs
- 4-5 dextrose tablets
- 4 jelly babies

If the child hasn't recovered after fifteen minutes and their blood glucose is still below 4, then repeat one of the treatments given above. As soon as your child feels better, then they should eat a starchy carbohydrate snack such as a sandwich or a banana or a usual meal, if it's mealtime.

Ring 999 immediately if

- Your child is unconscious.
- Your child is unable to eat or drink. Do *not* force food or drink down, as that could cause the child to choke.

CHAPTER 9

Glucagon Injection: You Might Never Need It, but Be Aware!

Eddie has had endless hypos in the last thirteen years. Some of them have been extremely worrying, but none have been as severe as the one we experienced a few weeks ago.

I went in to wake him up, in the morning and he was totally unresponsive. We missed his hypo, and it rendered Eddie unconscious. Therefore, he was physically unable to eat or drink a source of rapid glucose. Suddenly I wasn't in control, and my child was in a bad place.

I rang 999 in a total panic. I couldn't wait for the paramedics, so I decided to use the glucagon injection that had sat in my fridge for a while. (If you have one, check the use-by date regularly). I had never used it and never even opened the orange box to look inside. This injection basically tells the liver to release glucogen, which is converted into glucose, into the bloodstream and raise the blood-glucose level again. It can be a lifesaving treatment.

Believe me, I was scared. The needle was huge. But I knew I just had to get on with it. I injected Eddie's bottom and expected him to yelp, but he never felt a thing. Thankfully, the ambulance arrived, and the paramedics commended me on my quick thinking.

After treatment with several tubes of Glucogel and forty-five minutes later, Eddie finally came round. Afterwards, he felt very sick due to the glucagon injection, but this is a normal reaction.

Please do not use glucagon if your child is allergic to it.

CHAPTER 10

Sick Day Tips

Having a sick child is never easy, even at the best of times, but if your child has type 1 diabetes, then any sickness is a nightmare. Sometimes I only have to hear that one of Eddie's friends has a bug to panic and think about hospital admission. So, Eddie's sick days are a bit more severe than a runny nose and sneezes. A cold or flu or any other condition resulting in vomiting and diarrhoea may cause the blood glucose levels to rise, so it's very important to test these levels more often than usual when your child is sick. (Children with type 1 diabetes can automatically have a flu vaccination. Please ask your GP about this.)

When your child is ill:

- Their body will become resistant to insulin, so they will need more.
- Always continue to give your child insulin, even if they're not eating.
- Check blood glucose levels every two to four hours
- Give correction injections if blood glucose is high.
- Test for ketones if blood glucose levels are above 14 every two hours. Positive ketone tests *always* need treatment.
- Telephone your DSN or doctor if you are really worried.
- Fluids are essential. Make sure your child drinks plenty, even if only in sips through a straw.
- Dehydration can result from high blood glucose levels as your child goes to the toilet more. High blood glucose levels also usually happen if your child has a raised temperature with a cold or flu.
- If your child has a high temperature, paracetamol is essential. Speak to your doctor or pharmacist, If you need advice on dosages.
- Low blood glucose levels can occur with vomiting and diarrhoea.
- Long-acting insulin. Test often to see if short-acting insulin is also required. Your DSN can advise you.

Diet

If your child doesn't want to eat or drink normally, offer small frequent snacks of foods containing carbohydrates. Ice cream usually goes down well, and so does yogurt, soup, and milkshakes. If your child is vomiting and not able to eat, then give them small sips of sugary drinks to prevent low blood-glucose levels. A good guide (and only a guide) is to give fluids containing 10g of carbohydrates every hour if blood glucose levels are below 10 mmol. These are some sources:

- Lucozade (original), 60 ml
- Lucozade (sport), 150 ml
- Ribena, 75 ml
- Fanta, 75 ml
- Normal Coke *not diet*, 90 ml

Don't forget to also offer your child plenty of water or sugar-free squashes.

CHAPTER 11

Finger Pricking and Insulin Injections

When Eddie was young, giving him his injections was a battle. At two, he would run and hide under the table rather than let me give him his insulin. I hated that my child disliked it, I felt angry and sad, and I wanted diabetes to leave my baby alone. But, I had no choice. I had to enforce regular testing and I had to give regular insulin injections to my fearful child. I knew this was an essential part of his diabetes care for his long-term health.

So, what do you do to dispel the anger and frustration your child feels? I let Eddie know it was okay not to like what I was doing and that Mummy didn't like it either. I made sure I allowed Eddie to be upset. After all, at two years of age, he didn't understand why I had to constantly jab him in the thigh. I tried to explain, as well as you can to a toddler, that he needed these injections to keep him well and that if he didn't get them, he would get poorly and may have to go to hospital. If your child is older, you can explain that they will miss out on school, playing with their friends, or other activities if they miss their injections.

It's also important to get your child involved with their diabetes as soon as they're old enough. At first they can dial their insulin pens and read the numbers off the meter.

Above all, don't give up. *Never* skip testing or injections because your child is having a tantrum, and never negotiate. Their diabetes regime is a priority, and you have to be strong, in charge, and, above all, in control. If your child is seriously upset by the procedure, then turn to your DSN for help.

We had to get help with Eddie. Our diabetes clinic sent play leaders from the children's ward of the hospital to demonstrate insulin injections on Eddie's favourite teddies, and it actually helped. Here are some more tips for making injections easier:

- Get everything ready out of your child's sight, so they won't be aware of what's coming.
- For babies, give injections or do blood tests whilst feeding.
- Distract your child with a song, a story, or their favourite teddy or doll.
- Offer rewards. I used to give Eddie stickers for every finger prick and injection for the week and then, at the end of the week he would trade them in for some sort of prize.
- Praise your child and give them a hug.

- Make sure you have washed your hands and the injection site.
- Before administering insulin, I always used to do an air shot: I dial up two units and eject into the air to ensure the insulin reaches the tip of the needle.
- Choose a fatty site for injections, and put the needle in quickly.

- If your child finds injections uncomfortable or painful, then rub a piece of ice on the site for twenty seconds before an injection.
- Inject the insulin, make sure the button on the pen is pressed down fully, then count to 10 slowly, then remove the needle.
- Dispose of the needle safely.
- Dispose of any insulin that has been out of the fridge for twenty-eight days or more.

CHAPTER 12

Insulin Regime

I am not going to go into detail about different types of insulin, but I will mention them in a nutshell. First there is a long-acting or basal insulin, which is a background insulin that lasts approximately twenty-four hours. Each child will require a different dose based on his or her weight. This type is taken once a day or twice in some cases. Second is rapid or short-acting or bolus insulin. This insulin is given before or after meals and snacks, usually at least four times a day. The peak action lasts up to two hours, but in total it lasts between four and five hours. Last is mixed insulin, which is usually given to small children up to 5 years of age and only before breakfast and dinner. I found mixed insulin restricting, as it required Eddie to eat at nearly the same time of day every day and to have the same amount of carbohydrate each time. Very difficult with an inconsistent two-year-old! The rapid-acting insulin allows more flexibility with meal times and contents. Carbohydrate counting is usually done in addition to this regime to achieve better control.

Some children need more insulin at night because growth hormones and cortisol stimulate the liver to release extra glucose into the blood at this time of day. As a child gets older, the *dawn effect*, or an increased secretion of glucose in the early morning, comes into play.

Choosing the site for your child's insulin injection

Don't use the same site every time you inject.

- Move from site to site (use *site rotation*). If you continue to use the same site, then lumps can occur as tissue changes, preventing the amount or rate of absorption of insulin.
- Insulin enters the blood more quickly in some areas of the body than others:

Fastest

1. Stomach
2. Arms
3. Legs
4. Buttocks

Slowest

Of course, there is an exception to every rule! If you inject in your thighs and then exercise, the blood flow will increase to the legs, so insulin will be absorbed more quickly from that site than from the stomach.

Don't forget to put all needles in a sharps container!

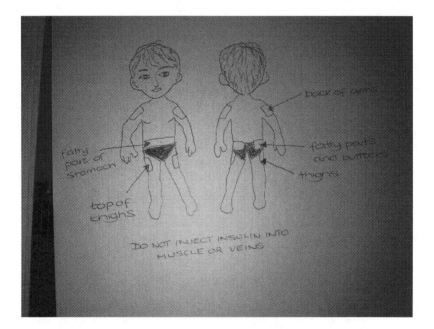

CHAPTER 13

Moving On to an Insulin Pump

An insulin pump is like an artificial pancreas, as it regularly delivers tiny doses of insulin, and it's small enough to fit in a child's pocket or clipped to a child's waistband. This device administers insulin through flexible tubing and a cannula into a layer of fat under the skin and replaces the need for injections. It can also administer boluses with a remote control, so you can still give your child insulin as they get down from the table! Many children, even babies as young as days old can use an insulin pump.

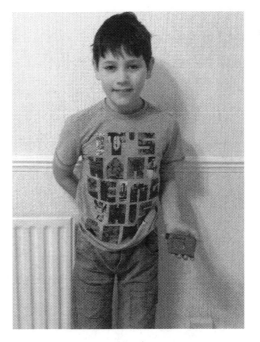

Most parents are glad to transition away from insulin pens, as it gives their children their childhoods back and gives the parents more flexibility with features such as temporary basals, bolus waving, and many others. There are currently seven insulin pumps available to choose from in the UK.

An insulin pump also provides much smaller doses than injections, so it's not only more accurate but also ideal for young children. The pump also enables parents to set different ratios for different times of the day.

Nevertheless, an insulin pump is not for the faint-hearted, and using one still requires commitment, as you will still need to:

- Regularly check your child's blood-glucose levels.
- Know how to count carbohydrates.
- Understand basic technology.
- Be motivated to help your child achieve maximum control.
- Have support from the whole family.

Advice for parents

I'm worried about my child going on a pump.

This is natural, but pumps are very well designed, sturdy, hard-wearing, and securely attached, so if your child is active or sporty, then have no fear. What I like about a pump is that the insulin can be stopped for up to an hour when your child is engaging in sports or other physical activities.

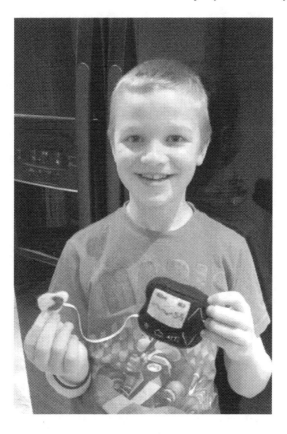

Will everyone know my child is wearing an insulin pump?

Insulin pumps are small and discreet and can be worn under clothes.

But my child wants to go swimming.

You can disconnect the pump for up to an hour, so no problems there. Just ensure that you randomly check your child's blood-glucose levels in the meantime.

Roxana Reynolds

I don't think my child will like the cannula, as the needle might hurt.

With the pumps currently on the market, no needles stay in the child. Instead, flexible tubing and cannulae deliver insulin under the skin. You change these every couple of days, and if you follow proper cleaning procedures, infections are rare.

Kelsie's transition to a pump

Kelsie was diagnosed at twenty months when she was in severe DKA. After a short time in the post-natal intensive care unit in Bristol, we were taken back to our local hospital to learn to care for her. The doctor put her on MDI, (multiple daily injections) Levemir, and Humalog at first, and the nurse mentioned the pump but then said she didn't want to overwhelm us with information, so she didn't mention it again for a few weeks. In the meantime, Kelsie took 3 units of Levemir per day and usually 0.5 units of Humalog with meals. We didn't count carbs then, just gave Kelsie insulin depending on how big the meal looked.

After a couple of weeks, the doctor dropped the Levemir dose to 1.5 units, but that was too high, and 1 unit was too low. Kelsie's bloods would go from the 20s down to 2 in 45 minutes, and we had no real control at all. A couple of months later, we added a teatime dose of Humulin M3 in an attempt to keep Kelsie's levels from being so high at night. At this point, she often had 6 injections a day, and her HbA1c was around 9 mmol/mol.

Our nurse and consultant had mentioned the pump several times by then, but I was very resistant, as I didn't want something attached to my child, and I was also scared of change. I soon realised, though, that something had to change, as we just couldn't go on as we were, and I agreed to the pump.

Kelsie got the pump a few weeks later, at the age of two years and five months. We had about two hours of training, and then the cannula was inserted. Kelsie didn't even flinch. We then popped the pump into her new cupcake-print pump pouch and went off to the hospital cafeteria for lunch. When we gave her the first bolus through the pump, it felt strange but wonderful that I didn't have to inject her. Even though she was very young, she seemed to understand that the pump meant no more injections, and she accepted it instantly. She never tried to take it off and has never complained about it. In fact, she actually gets quite protective of it, and she used to cry when we took it off for baths or to change her site.

As she was so young, the fact we could give her insulin in tiny doses changed our lives. Not only did her blood sugar become more stable, but she no longer needed to restrict her food intake. She could eat when she was hungry instead of having to eating according to a strict routine. She could now sleep in, unlike when she was on MDI and we had to get her up at 7 a.m. to have her Levemir and a meal to prevent her from being high all day. Now she could eat whatever snacks she wanted rather than having only carb-free or low-carb snacks. The ability to change the basals for different times of day was also great, as she needs almost no insulin at various times at school, but such variation wasn't possible on MDI. The pump has helped to prevent the horrible hypos and fast drops she was having.

I think the pump is especially great for small children like Kelsie, who need very small but accurate amounts of insulin. Kelsie still wears her pump in a pump pouch, and she has about fifteen of them. She also has a couple of Lycra bands to wear for gymnastics to keep the pump from bouncing around while she bounces. We all love the pump and really feel that it gave us our lives back after a very difficult few months struggling on MDI.

Isla's transition to a pump

I'm so grateful we got a pump for my eldest daughter, Isla, when we did. It's had such a positive impact on my little girl's standard of living.

Isla was diagnosed with type 1 diabetes at two years and ten months of age. The first therapy type we were put on was mixed injections, starting with two a day, morning and night. It didn't take long for this to change. Isla kept going low in the morning from the night-time injection, so we went down to one injection, in the morning. This was a nice way for Isla to ease into the whole injection thing, but it really didn't work for us. We felt like we were chasing the insulin all day. We gave her a daily dose in one hit in the morning, and then we had to adapt our and, more importantly, her behaviour all day to keep her levels in check. We had to say no to certain foods at certain times, and if she was ill or didn't want to eat, panic stations arose later in the day because she'd already had her insulin.

Next came MDI, which increased Isla's injection count to four a day-one with each meal and then the injection of long-acting insulin at bedtime. This helped us be more flexible with the ever-changing appetite of a three-year-old, but her poor little thighs suffered from so many jabs each day. She became quite bruised. She also hated having lift up her skirt or pull down her trousers straight after dinner in front of everyone, even at that young age. We didn't ever want her to feel like she had to hide, but she often got upset at even the thought of having to do it.

In addition, the pens we used for injections were limited in the increments of insulin they could administer, some only going up one unit at a time. For a person so tiny who needed such small doses of insulin, this often meant making the difficult decision between going slightly above the dose and risking a low or going slightly below the dose and risking a high.

Then, within the week of Isla's one-year anniversary of her diagnosis, we received funding for Isla to move to pump therapy. At first I found the thought unbearable that my baby would have to have something so visible attached to her all the time. Even during the training and when choosing a pump, I still struggled with the thought of her wearing it. It was only when my husband and I wore pumps ourselves for a trial week that I realised how lightweight and inconspicuous this device actually was and how little the cannulae hurt. As with all the changes Isla has gone through, she took to the pump like a duck to water. And as cheesy as it sounds, she got back some of her childhood freedom. We can now react to Isla's appetite and activity for the day rather than having to dictate these to match the insulin doses she's already been given. We can deliver far more accurate insulin doses because the pump can administer tiny doses—brilliant, especially for such a young child who needs so little insulin.

We can also adapt Isla's doses no matter what life throws at us. We can stop insulin immediately, we can increase it with temporary basal settings, and we can program specific profiles for days when she needs less insulin than others, such as PE days. We've also programmed different ratios for each part of the day. We learnt these ratios through trial and error, but imagine trying to remember all of them when carb counting on MDI! The pump's possibilities are endless. We are also currently learning when to use multi-wave and when to use extended bolus types to best match the breakdown of food to the progress of insulin.

Learning all these new techniques and technologies isn't without its challenges, but we see results so quickly that it's a joy to learn them for our little one. I'm no longer worried to let Isla join in or to try anything, as I know I can react to whatever happens. The pump really is the nearest thing we've got to the artificial pancreas, and I'm so grateful we got Isla's when we did. With Isla's pump, we controls her diabetes, her diabetes doesn't control us.

CHAPTER 14

How to Keep Your Child Active

Get active!

Physical activity is good for everyone, but it's even more important for those with diabetes.

Did you know?

Exercise not only helps to keep weight down but also makes children feel so much better. They sleep more soundly, have lower blood-glucose readings, and are more alert. This is why just walking to school is so beneficial. So get your child off the PlayStation or Xbox and get them moving!

Physical activity will keep your child's body healthy and strong and their weight stable. Because they'll be more alert, they'll learn better.

So how can I get my child moving?

Toddlers naturally have loads of energy, you just have to keep up!

Older children can become idle if you let them, so exercise is up to you. Walking is good, and so is cycling as a family. You can also get your child a skateboard, ice skates, or Rollerblades. Your child could join a gymnastics group, try boxing, join the local athletics club, or go swimming. There are numerous opportunities for golf, football, tennis, and any other sport they'd like.

What if I just haven't got a sporty child?

Here are a few ideas for activities that aren't sporty:

- Skipping whilst watching television (yes, I did say that!)
- Running up and down the stairs, possibly annoying the neighbours

- Helping with housework or gardening (you may have to pay your child)

Above all, exercise has got to be fun. Before your child does any exercise, check their blood-glucose level and have them to eat a small snack if necessary. Always keep something to hand, such as fruit juice, glucose tablets, Lucozade, or a carbohydrate snack to treat a hypo.

CHAPTER 15

The Sports Dilemma

There doesn't appear to be a right or wrong way to approach exercise, and all our children are different, so you'll have to figure it out for your child through trial and error.

Please discuss any concerns you have with your diabetes team, and remember as you read that *usually* does not mean *always*.

Start of exercise

Usually stop-start exercise causes blood glucose levels to rise, but this doesn't always happen. It depends on when your child last ate, when they had their insulin, and how many hours the dose will still be working. Because of settings for temporary basal rates and other factors, exercise isn't as daunting with an insulin pump.

If your child has insufficient insulin in the blood, then their blood-glucose levels are going to rise during exercise. This happens because stress hormones activated by exercise cause the liver to release glucose into the blood. The more intense the exercise, the more glucose the liver secretes. Blood sugars can rise due to dehydration, so make sure your child drinks plenty of water during exercise.

Continuous exercise

If your child is exercising for more than forty-five minutes without stopping, then there is a good chance a hypo could occur.

What to do:

Reduce the insulin dose by up to 50 per cent the usual amount at the meal before exercise.

Check blood sugar just before exercise. I like to see a reading of 10. If I see 7 or less, then I'll give Eddie a 15 g snack. This is just a guide; your child's levels will differ.

Let your child have a 15-30 g snack for each hour of exercise, eaten about 45 minutes before the start of exercise. Bananas on toast is a great snack.

Check the child's blood-glucose levels during exercise, and treat accordingly.

Check the child's blood-glucose levels after exercise. Be aware that blood sugars can continue to drop for even up to twelve hours after very strenuous exercise, so your child may need less insulin at meals after exercise.

A sporting inspiration

Alexander was diagnosed when he was five, and he is now nine. On diagnosis, he did poorly at all sports. His mum then withdrew him and started again with basics: First he had one-to-one tennis lessons and swimming lessons, and eventually he joined mainstream group lessons. Alexander has since swum a mile, his mum pushing glucose tablets into his mouth every 50 m. He finished with a blood-glucose level of 4!

He started rugby when he was seven, and initially he struggled, experiencing both hypoglycaemia and hyperglycaemia. This had a significant effect on him and his mum. The easiest thing would have been just to give up, but Alexander and his mum persevered, and two years later, Alexander has settled in to rugby.

Now, Alexander has just started golf lessons, and he also plays football and goes horse riding and kayaking, to name a few activities. There's no stopping him now. He has a can-do attitude, and diabetes does not stand in his way.

CHAPTER 16
Travelling Abroad

Travelling abroad with children is challenging enough, but it becomes daunting with children with type 1, and some parents just won't go. However, with proper preparation and plenty of planning and lists, travel shouldn't be a problem. You shouldn't put off a holiday abroad because your child has diabetes.

Eddie was diagnosed in the month of April, and we went abroad to Spain in June. Yes, travelling was hard, but we saw it as another challenge overcome.

Simple tips

- Ask your DSN for advice on insulin requirements. Eddie has always needed less when we've gone anywhere hotter than twenty-five degrees Celsius, as the heat can make insulin work more quickly.
- Ask for a letter from your DSN or GP outlining your child's diagnosis care plan, medical treatments, and prescriptions.
- Ask for extra supplies of insulin, tests strips, and, if your child has an insulin pump, cannulae and batteries and everything else the pump needs. Those with a pump shouldn't forget to take short—and long-acting insulin pens as well in case the pump stops working.
- Always put insulin in your hand luggage and *never* in the hold of a plane, as the insulin could freeze and become unusable.
- I carry all our insulin supplies and hypo treatments in a cool bag containing mini ice blocks. Some companies make bags specifically for insulin storage.
- You may be entitled to a European Health Insurance Card, which gives you access to reduced-cost medical treatment in the EU. An EHIC is available from your doctor and the post office.
- Dehydration raises blood glucose levels.

- Extreme temperatures can harm insulin, meters, and test strips, so keep them away from direct sunlight and never let them freeze.
- Have your child wear plastic sandals on the beach and water shoes in the sea as hot sand, broken glass, or sharp rocks can injure the feet.

Airport security and pumpers

- Twelve hours before your flight, change the pump cartridge/insulin, line, site, and battery. This will give you peace of mind that everything on your child's pump is working properly.
- You must remove jewellery, belts, and other accessories when going through a body scanner, but your child can leave their pump on.
- The X-ray scanner could damage an insulin pump, so if in any doubt, speak to someone in security before going through, and show them a letter from your diabetes clinic or doctor stating that your child has an insulin pump and its requirements.
- Security is not normally concerned about the small amount of insulin in the pump.

Pumps on planes

Pressure changes during flight will affect insulin delivery from your child's pump. When flying, you will need to:

- Check for bubbles regularly.
- Check that the pump is working properly, especially when at higher altitudes.

- If your child has a continuous glucose monitor (CGM), it can interfere with airline navigation equipment, so you must disconnect it before you enter the plane.

During the flight

- Your child should drink plenty of water.
- Check blood-glucose levels every two hours.
- Eat at regular meal times.
- Sleep when the plane turns the lights down.

Long-haul flights

- You'll be crossing time zones, so you'll have to change the pump's clock regularly to match what your child is doing. For example, when your child is sleeping for several hours, you'll need to put the pump in night mode, and when your child is going to eat, ensure that the pump is in the normal mode for mealtimes.
- We always carry a few snacks such as biscuits, crisps, dried fruit just in case.
- When you arrive at your destination, change the pump time to the local time.

Travel insurance

- Be sure you purchase insurance that covers any medical expenses and hospital admissions. You can shop online.
- Carry the company's contact details with you.
- Consider insuring your child's insulin pump, if they have one.

- For more travel tips and advice, please look at Diabetes Uk http://www.diabetes.uk and VogageMD: Advice for travelling with Diabetes http://www.voyagemd.com.

Packing list

- Letter from DSN/GP stating your child has diabetes
- Letter from DSN/GP stating your child has an insulin pump (if appropriate)
- Treatment for hypos (dextrose sweets, GlucoTabs, jelly babies, or similar, as liquids cannot be taken through passport control)
- Insulin in a clear plastic bag in hand luggage

Children that use injections

- Blood sugar meter
- Strips for meter
- Lancets for finger pricking
- Insulin pens
- Needles
- Short-acting insulin
- Long-acting insulin
- Hypo treatments
- Spare batteries

Children that use an insulin pump

- Infusion sets/cannulae
- Vials of insulin
- Spare batteries

- Blood sugar meter
- Lancets for finger pricking
- Insulin pens, insulin, and needles for an emergency
- Identity card, bracelet, band, or jewellery eg. Medic Alert or Wowbands
- First-aid kit containing sterile dressings, tape, and antiseptic cream, anti-diarrhoea tablets; simple analgesic tablets, and plasters

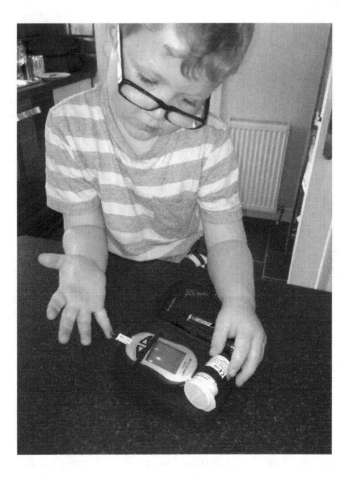

CHAPTER 17

Food and Your Child

Feeding a toddler is never easy, but feeding one with type 1 as well is a bit more of a problem. I think the food aspect is one of the hardest parts of coping with diabetes. Children's appetites change constantly, and they can be picky eaters and may suddenly dislike a food they've been eating for weeks. One thing I learnt early on with Eddie is despite the need to have a routine, you really can't enforce a strict meal plan. Eddie used to refuse to eat after I had given him his insulin, and this caused major upset and frustration for both of us.

What do you do when your child flatly refuses to eat?

I found that Eddie would take juice or milk (both a source of carbohydrates) most of the time. As juice is usually used to treat a hypo, please use it in moderation, or dilute it with water.

If your child really won't put anything in their mouth, then you'll have to watch for hypos vigilantly and treat them accordingly when they arise. Also be careful that your child doesn't develop starvation ketones from a lack of food and insulin, as ketones can occur with a low blood-glucose level. I can guarantee that your child will eventually get hungry, however. Do not put pressure on your child to eat, as this may cause a food issue.

I remember only too well how helpless I felt when Eddie refused to eat. Finally I spoke to our DSN, who advised, "Ask him what he wants to eat." After that, Eddie ate a lot of custard, even for breakfast! Of course we want our children to eat a healthy, balanced diet, and we all start out with good intentions, but when you see your child grimace, spit food out, get angry, and throw offending food on the floor, then you know that the battle has to stop and, in this instance, that you have to give in. This is especially hard if also you have other children, but that's another topic!

At the end of the day, children can be fussy eaters, and it's up to you to offer your children a variety of foods. We used to keep a reward chart for good eating habits, and sometimes it worked.

If you're experiencing severe problems, please speak with your diabetes clinic, as your child's insulin doses may need to be adjusted.

What are carbohydrates, or carbs?

Many of the foods we eat contain carbohydrates, or carbs. These are a source of energy that your child needs for growth and brain development. Carbs turn into glucose, and insulin is the key that moves the glucose to cells, where it's used for energy. This energy helps your child to walk, grow, play, and do all the other physical. Carbs are needed to fuel the brain with glucose to enable your child to learn.

So what foods contain carbs?

To name but a few:

- Bread
- Crackers
- Tortillas
- Pasta
- Noodles
- Cereal
- Grains

- Rice
- Couscous
- Potatoes
- Corn
- Peas
- Milk
- Yogurt
- Sweets
- Chocolate
- Cakes
- Biscuits
- Ice cream
- Fruit juices
- Non-diet drinks
- Smoothies
- Chips
- Pizza
- Spaghetti sauce
- Ketchup

Snack foods can be eaten as part of a balanced diet, but beware of their fat content.

No food is forbidden just because your child has type 1 diabetes, but you must be aware of what you choose to feed your child. Eating a healthy diet is as important to your overall diabetes care plan as testing blood-glucose levels, taking insulin, and engaging in physical activity.

Blood sugars affect health, mood, and energy. Rapid changes in blood sugars can trigger mood swings, hyperactivity, and concentration problems. Ideally, you should choose foods that raise blood sugars slowly. The glycemic index (GI) is a numerical value for a specific carbohydrate-containing food that shows how quickly that food can raise the blood sugar:

A GI of 70 or more = high GI
59-69 = medium GI
less than 55 = low GI.

High GI foods break down quickly, resulting in a rapid rise in blood sugar. Low GI foods take longer to break down, causing a slow, steady rise in blood sugar.

High GI foods

- Cakes, biscuits, pastries, and pies (and they're full of fat, too)
- Honey (full of sugar)
- Mashed potatoes and baked potatoes
- Cheerios
- Cornflakes
- Rice Krispies
- Coco Pops
- Long grain white rice
- White bread

- French bread

Medium GI foods

- Brown rice
- Raisins
- Bananas
- Sweet corn
- Special K cereal
- Instant porridge

Low GI foods

- Low-fat yogurt with no sugar
- Cheese strings
- Milk
- Pears, apples, plums, peaches and cherries and grapes
- Tomato soup
- Canned baked beans
- Pineapple juice
- Porridge
- Peanuts

Carbohydrate Counting

Counting carbs requires some maths. By law, foods have to show nutritional information on labels. To see the amount of carbs in your food, look at the amount of "Total carbohydrates" on the label, not "Sugars".

The carbohydrates will usually be given in amounts per 100 g, so you'll have to work out how many grams your child is going to eat. For example:

The food contains 64g per 100g

Your child eats 25g of that food

Your child will get 25 x 64 = 16g

Your DSN will calculate your child's insulin ration, based on their weight, height, age, and other factors. Here is an example for how to use this ratio:

If your child was given a ratio of 1:10, this means 1 unit of insulin to every 10g of carbs.

Using the earlier example of carbs, if your child was on a 1:10 ratio and ate 16g of carbs, they would need 1.5 units of insulin. With some insulin, this would be rounded to 1 or 2 units. With the insulin pump, the dosage can be more precise.

Initially you will have to look at every label, weigh everything you give your child to eat. but in time, you'll become familiar with your favourite foods and will instinctively know how many carbs are in them. *Carbs and Cals: A Visual Guide to Carbohydrate Counting* by Chris Cheyette and Yello Balolia is an invaluable resource. There's also a companion app for Apple and Android phones. You'll need a NutriScale, which tells you the amount of carbs in various foods. We use the Rosemary Conley NutriScale. However, when you eat out, you won't have your scales to hand, so a way to approximate is to refer to a woman's hand:

The palm, not including fingers and thumb = 85g of cooked or
boneless meat

A fist = 30g carb (ideal for jacket potatoes) Please note this is a
guide only.

A thumb = 1 tablespoon (1 serving of mayonnaise)

Thumb tip = 1 teaspoon

Basic carbohydrate portion guide

Medium slice of bread	15 g of carb
Medium bread roll	25 g
1-inch French stick	10 g
1 Weetabix	10 g
30 g cornflakes	25 g
30 g Rice Krispies	25 g
30 g chips (5 medium)	10 g
Medium apple/pear/orange	15 g
Medium banana	20 g
200 ml glass pure fruit juice	20 g
200 ml glass of milk	10 g
1 digestive biscuit	10 g
2 rich tea biscuits	10 g
2 Jaffa cakes	15 g
Doughnut	25 g
65 g standard Mars Bar	45 g
1 small (25 g) packet of crisps	15 g
50 ml Lucozade	10 g
3 dextrose tablets	10 g

So how many carbs should I give my child?

This is only a guide, as every child is different. Talk to your dietician
or DSN to get help deciding the right amount for your child.

- 5 years old: 30 to 45 g of carbs at each meal
- 5 to 12 years old: 45 to 60 g of carbs at each meal
- Teen boys: 60 to 75 g of carbs or more at each meal, plus regular snacks as they grow. Eddie has 100 g per meal.
- Teen girls: 45 to 75 g of carbs at each meal. Snacks be in the range of 15 to 30 g of carbs.

Your child's diet

I am not a nutritionist, but diet is common sense. Try to include:

- Fruit and vegetables (we all know the five-a-day rule). If your child really won't eat many of these, I've found smoothies to be invaluable. You can mix a base of milk or yogurt with almost any fruit, but don't forget to count the carbs.

- Protein, which is in meat, eggs, fish, beans, and nuts. These are essential for cell growth and repair and provide essential vitamins and minerals. Protein foods don't affect blood glucose levels.

- Milk and dairy. Children need this group to build strong bones and teeth. Dairy products provide calcium, energy, and protein. Most dairy products contain lactose, which is a natural milk sugar, so it will affect blood glucose levels. Cheese doesn't contain lactose, so it doesn't contain carbs.

- Fatty and sugary foods, such as crisps, sausages, sausage rolls, pastries, fried foods, sweets, cakes, chocolate, and biscuits. This is children's favourite group but it's a deluge of fat. Your child should have a minimum of these, as too much fat is not healthy, and even children can have high cholesterol levels. Butter, margarine, mayonnaise, salad cream, and cream should also be kept to a minimum. Fats do not raise blood-glucose levels, but they delay the digestion and absorption of sugar from carbs.

Other eating tips

Eating out with the family

Eating out can be worrying, but many restaurants have websites with nutritional information on them, enabling you to work out your child's carb content accurately.

Children's parties

You don't want your child to miss out, but you know they're going to eat more than usual at a party, and if you aren't going to be there, then you'll undoubtedly worry. You can ask the host what food is going to be on offer and also ask that they supervise your child. I used to go along with Eddie to parties until he was mature enough to make his own decisions. Eddie was about 9 but each child is different. Make sure that sugar free-drinks will also be available.

Treats

Children love sweets, but can you give your diabetic child sweets? We all know that too many aren't good for your child, but if your child's friends are eating them, the temptation is there. Eddie has never had sweets. He was two when he was diagnosed, so he didn't know any different, and my other son only had them as a treat once a week. It's up to you whether to give your child sweets. If you do, you can provide them after a main meal so they're included in your carb-to-insulin ratio. Eddie used to have chocolate as his treat, and I encouraged his grandparents and friends to buy him toy cars or magazines instead of sweets. I did allow sugar-free chewing gum, however.

CHAPTER 18

Nursery and Primary School

The day your child starts nursery or school is going to be one of the hardest days of your life, and I can guarantee you will be more upset than your child. Now that you have diabetes to contend, you'll worry how your child is going to get on. Who will provide blood testing and insulin doses? Will your child have a hypo?

Before that day, you'll speak to a head teacher or nursery leader, and representatives from your diabetes clinic may have gone in too, but if they don't, you can provide some information on diabetes such as what to look out so the head can pass it on to all relevant staff. You would be surprised how many adults know nothing about type 1 diabetes, so you'll need to ensure those caring for your child are educated.

Ideally, you should have a care plan for your child stating their name next to a picture so there is no doubt it is for your child. Everything mentioned below should be included in your plan:

- What time to give insulin doses, and how many units to give. Be aware that not every school will take the responsibility of providing these. I used to help as a dinner lady just so I could give Eddie his injections.
- Whether your child count carbs. If they do, put a sticker on their lunch box and write the amount of carbs in the lunch on it. If your child has school dinners, state whether they'll need help counting carbs.
- Who will help tests your child's blood-glucose level and what times tests should be done.
- Whether your child will need extra snacks and when (such as before PE and after PE).
- When your child can have optional snacks during the day.
- Signs of a hypo.
- How the staff should treat a hypo.

- What to do and who to ring of blood-glucose levels are high.
- Where your child's injections can be done.
- Contact details of parents and friends.
- A reminder to ring 999 and then you in an emergency.

Review this plan regularly, and keep open communication with your child's teachers. Keep a diary to share with your teacher. Supply the teacher with a box containing:

- Glucose tablets or sweets, Lucozade, GlucoGel, or other items to treat hypos.
- Snacks such as biscuits or cereal bars.
- If your child receives injections: Insulin and insulin pens, needles, and spares, and a reminder to keep insulin and insulin pens in the fridge.
- If your child has an insulin pump: Infusion sets, cannulae, tubing, batteries, spare insulin pens, insulin, and needles.
- Child's meter, test strips, and lancets.
- Sharps container such as a jar.

The box should be replenished regularly.

CHAPTER 19

I remember when

by Rosalin Midgeley

I remember when diabetes was just a word, when I could give you whatever you wanted to eat without thinking about carb counting and sugar content.

I remember that carefree smile you used to have, the spontaneous play you used to enjoy without having to test your blood to check if your levels are high enough to enjoy it or so low you have to sit and watch while you have something to eat!

I remember days out and holidays when we could just pile into the car and go, not have to make sure you had your insulin, testing kit, and enough snacks and hypo food.

I remember when the scariest things were the goblins and dragons in your bedtime stories. Now it's a monster called diabetes and his henchmen ketones and hypos that keep me awake to make sure they don't pay you a visit in the night.

I remember the day you were diagnosed, the fear in your eyes etched into my memory. I remember you were screaming you were sorry for being scared while I helped to hold you down for blood tests and a drip.

I remember how very brave you were when you realised you had to inject for the rest of your life.

I remember the first time you went to school with it. I had to hand your life over to someone who had only my written instructions to help keep you alive.

I remember how scared I was to let you do things other kids do, like go to parties and ride bikes in the park.

I remember how proud I am to be your mum each time someone says, "You can't do that! You're a diabetic!" and you go ahead and do it and succeed.

I am so proud of you for learning to live with diabetes and not letting it hold you back.

I look forward to all the years we will share and all the wonderful things you will achieve.

If I could take diabetes away from my three children and husband, I would. I remember life before diabetes, but only one of my children does.

CHAPTER 20

Serious Complications

Unfortunately, an awful lot of children with type 1 diabetes become complacent in their teens. My son has had his fair share of problems, but thankfully, our diabetes clinic has been extremely supportive, and just the simple act of talking to them has helped us enormously.

It's not cool to have diabetes, and a lot of adolescents don't want their friends knowing about their condition, so they often neglect their diabetes care. Mums often back off with their care, too, as their children become more responsible, but they sometimes back off too quickly, leaving their children to feels like they're in very deep water as the realise what diabetes really is and what a constant pain care is.

Eddie gave up eating breakfast and skimped on lunch so that he didn't have to inject insulin. This resulted in starvation ketones from lack of insulin and then weight loss, as Eddie peed out all the calories he took in. This went on for a while, and had it continued, Eddie could have developed serious complications.

Yes, diabetes care is hard, and realising that this disease is for life, unless there's a cure, can be depressing for your teen. One thing I've learnt is that however big and grown up your child seems, they still need support. If your teen suddenly can't be bothered with diabetes or becomes complacent and you can't get through to them, ask your DSN to help, even if the DSN recommends that your child speak to a psychologist.

Fact: Neglect and bad care = future complications.

**My rebellious youth
by Zara**

When I was small, my parents told me that I wasn't much different from anybody else. This wasn't true. They had always tried to bring me up the same as my brothers, but this was often impossible because of my ever erratic glucose levels.

This is not to say my parents' control of my illness was sloppy; quite the opposite. My parents were quite strict with my diabetes care and did everything that the specialists, dieticians, health visitors, and DSNs demanded, but still my HbA1c remained high and hypos struck when they felt like it. Only years later would I be diagnosed with diabetes-associated depression.

My depression started as early as primary school. My classmates did not understand my diabetes, and because of this, they cruelly and viciously bullied me. They would dangle their sweets in front of my face, telling me that I couldn't have them; they stole my hypo treatments; they told other children that I was a drug addict; and they broke my blood meters, amongst other things. I resented my illness, and I hated my body. I wished that it had happened to my brothers and not to me.

After many appeals, my application to the secondary school of my choice was accepted. I was keen to go to the school, as I had discovered that they had experience with diabetic pupils. This very reason meant that for once, I wouldn't have to rely on my parents. Most of the teachers knew how to handle hypos, so my parents were reluctant but happy to give me almost full control of my diabetes. The bullying continued, but it wasn't as severe as it had been at primary school.

My HbA1c was still high, and my hypos still attacked without warning. My specialists accused me of stuffing my face with sweets. This was not the case, but eventually, seeing as there was no improvement with my erratic blood glucose levels, I decided that as my specialists had already decided I was filling my face with sweets, I might as well do as they had decided. I also stopped testing my glucose levels, purely as a rebellious act. Although my parents had said they would give me most of the control of my diabetes, they were forever interfering and taking over, one of the many reasons of my rebellion.

Throughout my teens, I received minimal support from my diabetes team, and my rebellion carried on all the way through. At sixteen I was diagnosed with retinopathy after my consultant found that I was bleeding in the back of my right eye.

Just after my seventeenth birthday, I was rushed into hospital. I had developed tonsillitis a few weeks before, and I still was not testing my glucose levels, so when the vomiting started, I didn't give it a thought. I was ill, and I usually expect vomit when I'm ill. By the time I saw my GP, I was too weak to walk unaided. My parents had to carry me to hospital. Every inch of my body ached, and I had no idea where I was.

The diagnosis was severe DKA, and according to the doctors at the hospital, I was hours away from a coma.

When they eventually released me, I had learnt so much about my illness. I had never understood how quickly diabetes could turn on you. I knew that I had a shorter life expectancy, but I never knew how much shorter it could be.

Another year passed, and my legs started to cause problems. It started with very painful cramping travelling down my legs only took place at night. I was unable to sleep, as my legs hurt so very much. But being as headstrong as I was, I only consulted my specialist when I began losing feeling in my toes. I was then diagnosed with peripheral neuropathy. At this stage, the feeling that my body hated me was overwhelming.

I know a lot of people think that I brought most of it on myself, but they don't understand that my depression caused me to hate myself. I wasn't officially diagnosed with depression until after I had turned twenty, and then I insisted I could manage.

At twenty-one, my neuropathy became unbearably painful. My consultant recommended amitriptyline hydrochloride, an antidepressant proven to stimulate the peripheral nerves and reduce the pain caused by neuropathy. What I didn't know is that antidepressants can make depression much worse. After two weeks, I had to stop taking them.

My diabetes trapped me. My life wasn't mine, it belonged to my specialists and overprotective relatives. The year before, an aunt had made me swear on my grandfather's grave that I would get my act together and control it. I felt guilty that I had failed and betrayed my grandfather's memory. I was in a relationship that was going nowhere, and none of my friends understood any of what I was going through. I wished I had never been born, and I was desperate for a way out.

I dialled the pen containing my quick-acting insulin a far as it would go and jabbed it into my stomach. I took my breath and . . .

Nothing. My pen jammed the moment I tried to push in the fatal dose. The lethal injection I had prepared blatantly refused to be injected. I became frustrated and angry and threw the wretched device across the room.

In the moment the pen smashed against the wall, I realised that this wasn't me. I'd never put my own mother through the loss of another child. I remembered what losing my baby brother did to her. My grandfather would never forgive me for taking my life purely because I felt I'd disappointed his memory.

I stopped taking the antidepressants and asked my consultant for help. He referred me to psychotherapy, and the care for my diabetes became constant and far more supportive. I was also given the choice to see a DAFNE-qualified dietician instead of my consultant, thus creating consistency that my care had lacked.

Although it has taken me over twenty years, I have finally taken control of my illness and stopped it from controlling me. I still struggle with my depression and complications, but I have now developed a new will to live.

So what are the complications?

You won't want to think about what can happen to your child if their diabetes isn't controlled, but if you know what can occur, you know why you do everything you can to prevent them happening. I would like to add that your child will have regular health checks throughout their life, and any changes will be identified and treated accordingly, usually early. Health outcomes are considerably better than they used to be.

If your child's is HbA1c is usually good and your child has good control, then complications are greatly reduced and possibly prevented. Complications don't happen overnight. They are silent and gradual. They can take years to appear. Don't ever become complacent about your child's control, as your child could develop disabling or even life-threatening complications of the heart, blood vessels, nerves, eyes, or kidneys.

Here is a short list of what could happen:

Neuropathy (nerve damage)

Too much glucose in the blood can damage the walls of the capillaries, or smallest blood vessels. These nourish the nerves, especially in the legs. Symptoms are numbness, tingling, burning, and pain.

Nephropathy (kidney damage)

Diabetes can damage the tiny blood vessels that filter waste products from blood in the kidneys. High blood-glucose levels can result in cystitis and bladder and kidney infections.

Retinopathy (eye damage)

Blood vessels of the retina can be damaged over time by high blood-glucose levels. If left untreated, it can cause blindness. After your child is twelve, they will have an annual eye screening.

Heart and blood vessel diseases

Problems such as angina, heart attack, stroke, or high blood pressure can occur later in life.

Foot damage

Cuts and blisters can become infected if there is poor blood flow or nerve damage in the feet.

Periodontal disease (gum disease)

Children with diabetes can develop gum disease if they:

- Produce too much plaque and don't remove it adequately.
- Have constantly high blood-glucose levels, which leads to increased sugar in the mouth and poor circulation in the gums

The symptoms of gum disease include:

- bleeding and sensitive gums
- receding gums
- discoloured gums
- painful gums

To prevent this condition, manage blood glucose levels, brush and floss daily, and see a dentist regularly.

Foot care

Eddie often gets blisters. Thankfully, he doesn't have nerve damage in his feet, but high blood-glucose levels can cause nerve damage (neuropathy) that can affect the legs and feet. Children who have this condition might feel pain, tingling, even hot or cold. The consequence of having foot injuries with nerve damage is that your child may be unaware of sores spots, so they could get a whole lot worse, especially as high blood-glucose will feed the germs in the sore over time. Also, poor blood flow (peripheral vascular disease) means an infection or sore will take longer to heal. This is why it is paramount to achieve tight control.

A bad infection that doesn't heal can even develop into gangrene, which occurs when the tissue around a sore dies. This then blackens and becomes smelly. In severe cases, amputation is necessary. To prevent these complications:

- Wash your child's feet in warm water every day. Dry between the toes well, and add talc if you want.

- Check your child's feet every day for sores, cuts, blisters, redness, or any other problems.
- File any corns or hard skin with an emery board or pumice stone after a warm bath or shower. Avoid corn and callous removers. Consult a podiatrist, a doctor who specialises in feet if you have any concerns.
- Cut your child's toenails regularly, straight across and not too short. Cut after washing when the nails are soft.
- Make sure your child wears shoes that fit well to prevent blisters.
- Your child's feet should be examined by a GP or a diabetic professional at least once a year.

Common foot problems

High blood glucose levels + foot problems can = infection

- Corns and calluses, which are thick layers of skin, can become infected.
- Ingrowing toenails, which can result from tight-fitting shoes. These can get infected.
- Dry skin, as it can lead to cracks that germs can enter and cause infection.
- Athlete's foot, a fungus that causes redness, cracking of the skin, and itchiness.

If you have any doubt about a foot issue, please make an appointment to see your GP.

CHAPTER 21

History of Diabetes

If Eddie and I had lived one hundred years ago, neither of us would be here now. A horrible thought, but it's true. In the past, there was no treatment for diabetes; you just wasted away to a certain death. Until the twentieth century, diabetes mellitus, or "honeyed diabetes", was diagnosed by tasting the patient's urine to see if it was sweet! Thankfully, things changed.

In 1921 Frederick Banting, from Canada, and his assistant Charles Best kept a diabetic dog alive for seventy days by injecting it with some sort of concoction from a dog's pancreas. A few dogs were sacrificed in their research to discover insulin. Eventually, after a bit of refining, this injection was given to a young boy dying from diabetes. Within twenty-four hours, he had greatly improved. This indeed was a miracle and one of the first instances of treatment with insulin.

In 1919 Elizabeth Hughes 11 year old daughter of politician Charles Evans Hughes had been diagnosed with juvenile diabetes. Back then it was a death sentence. The only treatment was starvation which resulted in Elizabeth becoming skin and bone and weighing only 45 pounds!

Elizabeth was one of the first diabetics to receive insulin injections and lived until she was 70 years of age.

Medical breakthroughs continued:

- In 1935, Roger Hinsworth discovered that there were two types of diabetes, which he called "insulin sensitive" and "insulin insensitive".
- In the mid-1930s, pork and beef insulin was marketed.
- In the 1960s, urine test strips were developed to test blood glucose levels.
- In 1966 Anton H (Tom) Clemens started work on a blood glucose meter.
- In 1968 he built several prototypes for trials and filed a patent application.
- In September 1971 he was issued his first patent. Two years later it went on the market and could only be obtained by prescription. It was six and a half inches tall by four inches wide and weighed nearly two pounds.
-
- In 1979, HbA1c was devised.
- In the 1980s, synthetic insulin replaced insulin from cows, horses, pigs, or fish.
- In1982, Eli Lily marketed the first human insulin, Humulin.

In 1963, the first insulin pump was designed by Dr Arnold Kadish. It was huge and had to be worn as a backpack. Adjusting the insulin doses in some old pumps required a screwdriver. Just a bit inaccurate! It wasn't until the late 1980s and early '90s that things really improved and insulin pumps became more user friendly. After that, technology has developed at an alarming rate, and insulin pumps have gotten even smaller, more precise, and more beneficial for users.

Research is currently being conducted into a combination of electronic devices that work together to monitor and adjust insulin levels just like the pancreas does in people without diabetes. Trials haven't yet been done. Researchers are also using vaccine-type approaches to prevent type 1 diabetes from developing, meaning that eventually, we may see an end to type 1 diabetes.

Restaurants with Nutritional Information, Including Carbohydrate Content, on Their Websites

Burger King: burgerking.co.uk/nutrition

Harvester: Harvester.co.uk/nutrition

KFC: KFCco.uk/our food/meals/original-recipe-meal

McDonald's: McDonalds.com/get nutrition/nutritionfacts.pdf

Pizza Hut: pizza hut.co.uk/delivery/nutritional info.aspx

Subway: subwayco.uk; go to the menu, then click on "Nutritional Value"

Glossary

beta cell—the cells that produce insulin in the islets of Langerhans in the pancreas

basal—long-acting insulin

bolus—short-acting insulin

BG—blood glucose

blood-glucose meter—a device for measuring blood-glucose levels on the blood testing strips.

carbohydrates—a group of foods containing sugars and starches to give the body energy.

CGM—continuous glucose monitor

coma—a condition in which one is unconscious, unresponsive

complications—problems that can be caused by inadequate diabetes control cortisol—a hormone that affects blood sugar levels in the body.

DSN—diabetes specialist nurse

DKA—diabetic ketoacidosis, a dangerous complication caused by a severe lack of insulin, leaving the body unable to use glucose for energy.

glucagon—an injection for treating severe hypoglycaemia. This hormone releases glycogen from the liver to raise blood glucose levels.

honeymoon phase—a time when a small amount of insulin is still being produced by the pancreas. This usually lasts only a few months.

hyperglycaemia—high blood glucose, above 10 mmol/1

hypoglycaemia—low blood glucose, below 3.5 mmol/1. Abbreviated to *hypo*

insulin—a hormone produced by the beta cells of the pancreas to control blood-glucose levels. Can be given by injections or an insulin pump.

insulin pen—a device like a pen containing a cartridge of insulin. The dose is dialled, a button pressed, and insulin is released.

ketoacidosis—a dangerous complication caused by a severe lack of insulin, leaving the body unable to use glucose for energy. This results from fat in the body being used for energy and producing ketones as a by-product.

ketoacid—a compound formed when body fat is used to give the body energy. Acetone is one of these compounds.

lipohypertrophy—fatty lumps caused by repeated injections at the same site

MDI—multiple dose injections

nephropathy—kidney damage that makes the kidney leak. Can be serious if left untreated.

neuropathy—damage to the nerves.

pancreas—a gland situated behind the stomach that secretes pancreatic juice (a digestive fluid) and produces the hormones insulin and glucagon.

protein—a molecule found in high amounts in fish, meat, eggs, and milk that is essential for the repair of tissues and growth

retinopathy—damage to the retina, a structure at the back of the eye

Afterthought

I hope you have enjoyed reading this book and that it will give you the support you need to help your child.

Please try to remain positive. Your child will pick up on your emotions, so if you have a negative attitude and show despair or resentment, your child may feel bad about themselves and their diabetes.

I have often cried over diabetes and despaired, but I've never allowed my son to really see me cry; I've done that in private. The consequence of this is that my son does not hate diabetes, he views it as merely an inconvenience. Hating diabetes will stop you getting on. Oh yes, diabetes is a massive challenge, but my son and I are ready for it—we are armed with knowledge, we are empowered, we know we can cope.

Mums and Dads, this is just the beginning. Good luck.

If Only You Knew

by Sandra Murray

Hi, hello, how are you?

Oh my God, if only you knew.

I've been awake all night, worried and scared,

Constantly checking glucose levels to see how they fair.

One night they are high and we need to inject,

Then for the rest of the night I've to watch over and protect.

Another night when numbers fall,

And you don't wake is the most worrying of all.

It's always here, day in, day out,

Never a day off, not even time out.

As people lay sleeping, our friends and neighbours unaware.

I'm wide awake, having to give 24/7 care.

Diabetes does not switch off, not even at night.

At times we feel like we're up against an unbeatable fight.

I pray to God it will disappear from my little child's body,

He doesn't deserve this, not him, not anybody.

I won't let you take him, I've seen you try it before,

We'll stand up and fight you, now and for evermore.

Roxana Reynolds

You picked on the wrong son
By Nina Bailey

2 years ago you knocked on our door,
You took over his body,
Right to his core.
He was all skin and bone
No strength left within.
To fight against you and he nearly gave in.
You were killing him slowly,
He was wasting away.
You thought you had won.
But I am proud to say
You picked on the wrong son that very day.

See, he is a fighter of the toughest kind.
Although he fights quietly and with such pride.
He just needed one tool to help him beat you.
Insulin is his life saver . . . . it's his super glue!

So D, up yours, cos we have won.
My son is still here but I wish you were gone.
I wish I could sleep without a care in the world,
Without your constant reminder that you are still there.

Ready and waiting, always there, just to scare.
I wish he could eat without a seconds thought.
And that hypos and hypers wouldn't need our support.
No worrying and stressing about the simple things in life.
Just leave him be and let him strive.

So D, when you picked on my boy didn't you know,
He's the toughest one there is,
So you may as well just go.

You had not counted on this and for that I am sure.
And one day finally . . . . we will get a cure!

Useful Websites

https://www.pumpfashion.com/shop/ Pump Fashion

Debbie's son AJ was diagnosed with type 1 diabetes just after his fifteenth birthday. When he was twenty, she found out about insulin pumps through my social networking group on Facebook, she researched pumps, and she realised that AJ met the NICE criteria to have one, but her local hospital were not offering them to their patients. So, she started her own battle against the hospital and the PCT, and, with the help of INPUT, managed to get AJ an insulin pump six months later. The pump changed his life, but she couldn't find pump packs that he liked sold anywhere in the UK, as most of the companies seemed to focus on younger children. So, she formed a partnership with Pumpwear, Inc., in America and now very successfully runs Pumpfashion. They sell all types of pump packs and accessories, and have a nice selection of packs and meter cases that appeal to teenagers and adults.

http://www.wowbands.co.uk/ Wowbands

Funky and affordable medical-ID wristbands, hypo-kit bags, diabetes car signs, and key rings. Wowbands was founded in April 2010 by Melanie James. She started as a small online business and it has gradually grown, increased it's product range and has built up a loyal and highly valued customer base.

http://www.funkypumpers.com/

http://www.dia-wipe.com/

Funky Pumpers was launched in January 2011 by mum Sabrina Dawe after her son was diagnosed with type 1 diabetes aged just thirteen months. Funky Pumpers was the first company in the UK to specialise in insulin-pump accessories and now sell a wide variety of diabetes-related accessories as well as Dia-wipe, finger wipes used before blood-glucose testing

http://www.pumppitz.co.uk Pump-Pitz

Linsey's youngest daughter Betsy was diagnosed with type 1 9 days before her second birthday. Betsy coped really well with injections but her blood sugar levels would not stabalise even though she was having up to 10 injections a day. In April 2011 she finally got the funding for Betsy to go on an insulin pump. Her pump came with a clip that attached to her clothes but as she is a very lively girl it wasn't suitable so she decided to create a bag just for Betsy's pump. Pump-Pitz was created.

http://www.diabetes.org.uk/

http://www.jdrf.org.uk/